HISTORICAL RECORD

OF

THE SIXTEENTH,

OR,

THE BEDFORDSHIRE REGIMENT OF FOOT;

CONTAINING

AN ACCOUNT OF THE FORMATION OF THE REGIMENT

IN 1688,

AND OF ITS SUBSEQUENT SERVICES

TO 1848.

COMPILED BY

RICHARD CANNON, Esq.

ADJUTANT-GENERAL'S OFFICE, HORSE GUARDS.

The Naval & Military Press Ltd

Published by

The Naval & Military Press Ltd
Unit 10 Ridgewood Industrial Park,
Uckfield, East Sussex,
TN22 5QE England

Tel: +44 (0) 1825 749494
Fax: +44 (0) 1825 765701

www.naval-military-press.com
www.military-genealogy.com
www.militarymaproom.com

In reprinting in facsimile from the original, any imperfections are inevitably reproduced and the quality may fall short of modern type and cartographic standards.

GENERAL ORDERS.

HORSE-GUARDS,
1st *January*, 1836.

His MAJESTY has been pleased to command that, with the view of doing the fullest justice to Regiments, as well as to Individuals who have distinguished themselves by their Bravery in Action with the Enemy, an Account of the Services of every Regiment in the British Army shall be published under the superintendence and direction of the Adjutant-General; and that this Account shall contain the following particulars, viz.:—

—— The Period and Circumstances of the Original Formation of the Regiment; The Stations at which it has been from time to time employed; The Battles, Sieges, and other Military Operations in which it has been engaged, particularly specifying any Achievement it may have performed, and the Colours, Trophies, &c., it may have captured from the Enemy.

—— The Names of the Officers, and the number of Non-Commissioned Officers and Privates Killed or Wounded by the Enemy, specifying the place and Date of the Action.

GENERAL ORDERS.

——— The Names of those Officers who, in consideration of their Gallant Services and Meritorious Conduct in Engagements with the Enemy, have been distinguished with Titles, Medals, or other Marks of His Majesty's gracious favour.

——— The Names of all such Officers, Non-Commissioned Officers, and Privates, as may have specially signalized themselves in Action.

And,

——— The Badges and Devices which the Regiment may have been permitted to bear, and the Causes on account of which such Badges or Devices, or any other Marks of Distinction, have been granted.

By Command of the Right Honorable

GENERAL LORD HILL,
Commanding-in-Chief.

JOHN MACDONALD,
Adjutant-General.

PREFACE.

THE character and credit of the British Army must chiefly depend upon the zeal and ardour by which all who enter into its service are animated, and consequently it is of the highest importance that any measure calculated to excite the spirit of emulation, by which alone great and gallant actions are achieved, should be adopted.

Nothing can more fully tend to the accomplishment of this desirable object than a full display of the noble deeds with which the Military History of our country abounds. To hold forth these bright examples to the imitation of the youthful soldier, and thus to incite him to emulate the meritorious conduct of those who have preceded him in their honorable career, are among the motives that have given rise to the present publication.

The operations of the British Troops are, indeed, announced in the "London Gazette," from whence they are transferred into the public prints: the achievements of our armies are thus made known at the time of their occurrence, and receive the tribute of praise and admiration to which they are entitled. On extraordinary occasions, the Houses of Parliament have been in the habit of conferring on the Commanders, and the Officers and Troops acting under their orders, expressions of approbation and of thanks for their skill and bravery; and these testimonials, confirmed by the high ·honour of their Sovereign's approbation, constitute the reward which the soldier most highly prizes.

It has not, however, until late years, been the practice (which appears to have long prevailed in some of the Continental armies) for British Regiments to keep regular records of their services and achievements. Hence some difficulty has been experienced in obtaining, particularly from the old Regiments, an authentic account of their origin and subsequent services.

This defect will now be remedied, in consequence of His Majesty having been pleased to command that every Regiment shall, in future, keep a full and ample record of its services at home and abroad.

From the materials thus collected, the country will henceforth derive information as to the difficulties and privations which chequer the career of those who embrace the military profession. In Great Britain, where so large a number of persons are devoted to the active concerns of agriculture, manufactures, and commerce, and where these pursuits have, for so long a period, being undisturbed by the *presence of war*, which few other countries have escaped, comparatively little is known of the vicissitudes of active service and of the casualties of climate, to which, even during peace, the British Troops are exposed in every part of the globe, with little or no interval of repose.

In their tranquil enjoyment of the blessings which the country derives from the industry and the enterprise of the agriculturist and the trader, its happy inhabitants may be supposed not often to reflect on the perilous duties of the soldier and the sailor,—on their sufferings,—and on the sacrifice of valuable life, by which so many national benefits are obtained and preserved.

The conduct of the British Troops, their valour, and endurance, have shone conspicuously under great and trying difficulties; and their character has been established in Continental warfare by the irresistible spirit with which they have effected debarkations in spite of the most formidable opposition, and by the gallantry and steadiness with which they have maintained their advantages against superior numbers.

In the official Reports made by the respective Commanders, ample justice has generally been done to the gallant exertions of the Corps employed; but the details of their services and of acts of individual bravery can only be fully given in the Annals of the various Regiments.

These Records are now preparing for publication, under his Majesty's special authority, by Mr. RICHARD CANNON, Principal Clerk of the Adjutant General's Office; and while the perusal of them cannot fail to be useful and interesting to military men of every rank, it is considered that they will also afford entertainment and information to the general reader, particularly to those who may have served in the Army, or who have relatives in the Service.

There exists in the breasts of most of those who have served, or are serving, in the Army, an *Esprit de Corps*—an attachment to everything belonging to their Regiment; to such persons a narrative of the services of their own Corps cannot fail to prove interesting. Authentic accounts of the actions of the great, the valiant, the loyal, have always been of paramount interest with a brave and civilized people. Great Britain has produced a race of heroes who, in moments of danger and terror, have stood " firm as the rocks of their native shore :" and when half the world has been arrayed against them, they have fought the battles of their Country with unshaken fortitude. It is presumed that a record of achievements in war,—victories so complete and surprising, gained by our countrymen, our brothers, our fellow citizens in arms,—a record which revives the memory of the brave, and brings their gallant deeds before us, will certainly prove acceptable to the public.

Biographical memoirs of the Colonels and other distinguished Officers will be introduced in the Records of their respective Regiments, and the Honorary Distinctions which have, from time to time, been conferred upon each Regiment, as testifying the value and importance of its services, will be faithfully set forth.

As a convenient mode of Publication, the Record of each Regiment will be printed in a distinct number, so that when the whole shall be completed, the Parts may be bound up in numerical succession.

INTRODUCTION

TO

THE INFANTRY.

THE natives of Britain have, at all periods, been celebrated for innate courage and unshaken firmness, and the national superiority of the British troops over those of other countries has been evinced in the midst of the most imminent perils. History contains so many proofs of extraordinary acts of bravery, that no doubts can be raised upon the facts which are recorded. It must therefore be admitted, that the distinguishing feature of the British soldier is INTREPIDITY. This quality was evinced by the inhabitants of England when their country was invaded by Julius Cæsar with a Roman army, on which occasion the undaunted Britons rushed into the sea to attack the Roman soldiers as they descended from their ships; and, although their discipline and arms were inferior to those of their adversaries, yet their fierce and dauntless bearing intimidated the flower of the Roman troops, including Cæsar's favourite tenth legion. Their arms consisted of spears, short swords, and other weapons of rude construction. They had chariots, to the axles of which were fastened sharp pieces of iron resembling scythe-blades, and infantry in long chariots resembling waggons, who alighted and fought on foot, and for change of ground, pursuit or retreat, sprang into the chariot and drove off with the speed of cavalry. These inventions were, however, unavailing against Cæsar's legions: in the course of time a military system, with discipline and subordination, was introduced, and British courage, being thus regulated, was exerted to the greatest advantage; a full development of the national character followed, and it shone forth in all its native brilliancy.

The military force of the Anglo Saxons consisted principally of infantry: Thanes, and other men of property, however, fought on horseback. The infantry were of two classes, heavy and light. The former carried large shields armed with spikes, long broad swords and spears; and the latter were armed with swords or spears only. They had also men armed with clubs, others with battle-axes and javelins.

The feudal troops established by William the Conqueror consisted (as already stated in the Introduction to the Cavalry) almost entirely of horse; but when the warlike barons and knights, with their trains of tenants and vassals, took the field, a proportion of men appeared on foot, and, although these were of inferior degree, they proved stout-hearted Britons of stanch fidelity. When stipendiary troops were employed, infantry always constituted a considerable portion of the military force;

and this *arme* has since acquired, in every quarter of the globe, a celebrity never exceeded by the armies of any nation at any period.

The weapons carried by the infantry, during the several reigns succeeding the Conquest, were bows and arrows, half-pikes, lances, halberds, various kinds of battle-axes, swords, and daggers. Armour was worn on the head and body, and in course of time the practice became general for military men to be so completely cased in steel, that it was almost impossible to slay them.

The introduction of the use of gunpowder in the destructive purposes of war, in the early part of the fourteenth century, produced a change in the arms and equipment of the infantry-soldier. Bows and arrows gave place to various kinds of fire-arms, but British archers continued formidable adversaries; and owing to the inconvenient construction and imperfect bore of the fire-arms when first introduced, a body of men, well trained in the use of the bow from their youth, was considered a valuable acquisition to every army, even as late as the sixteenth century.

During a great part of the reign of Queen Elizabeth each company of infantry usually consisted of men armed five different ways; in every hundred men forty were "*men-at-arms*," and sixty "*shot*;" the "men-at-arms" were ten halberdiers, or battle-axe men, and thirty pikemen; and the "shot" were twenty archers, twenty musketeers, and twenty harquebusiers, and each man carried, besides his principal weapon, a sword and dagger.

xii INTRODUCTION

Companies of infantry varied at this period in numbers from 150 to 300 men; each company had a colour or ensign, and the mode of formation recommended by an English military writer (Sir John Smithe) in 1590 was:—the colour in the centre of the company guarded by the halberdiers; the pikemen in equal proportions, on each flank of the halberdiers: half the musketeers on each flank of the pikes; half the archers on each flank of the musketeers, and the harquebusiers (whose arms were much lighter than the muskets then in use) in equal proportions on each flank of the company for skirmishing.* It was customary to unite a number of companies into one body, called a REGIMENT, which frequently amounted to three thousand men: but each company continued to carry a colour. Numerous improvements were eventually introduced in the construction of fire-arms, and, it having been found impossible to make armour proof against the muskets then in use (which carried a very heavy ball) without its being too weighty for the soldier, armour was gradually laid aside by the infantry in the seventeenth century: bows and arrows also fell into disuse, and the infantry were reduced to two classes, viz.: *musketeers*, armed with matchlock muskets,

---

* A company of 200 men would appear thus :—

20	20	20	30	20	30	20	20	20
Harquebuses.	Archers.	Muskets.	Pikes.	Halberds.	Pikes.	Muskets.	Archers.	Harquebuses.

The musket carried a ball which weighed $\frac{1}{10}$th of a pound; and the harquebus a ball which weighed $\frac{1}{25}$th of a pound.

swords, and daggers; and *pikemen*, armed with pikes from fourteen to eighteen feet long, and swords.

In the early part of the seventeenth century Gustavus Adolphus, King of Sweden, reduced the strength of regiments to 1000 men. He caused the gunpowder, which had heretofore been carried in flasks, or in small wooden bandoliers, each containing a charge, to be made up into cartridges, and carried in pouches; and he formed each regiment into two wings of musketeers, and a centre division of pikemen. He also adopted the practice of forming four regiments into a brigade; and the number of colours was afterwards reduced to three in each regiment. He formed his columns so compactly that his infantry could resist the charge of the celebrated Polish horsemen and Austrian cuirassiers; and his armies became the admiration of other nations. His mode of formation was copied by the English, French, and other European states; but so great was the prejudice in favour of ancient customs, that all his improvements were not adopted until near a century afterwards.

In 1664 King Charles II. raised a corps for sea-service, styled the Admiral's regiment. In 1678 each company of 100 men usually consisted of 30 pikemen, 60 musketeers, and 10 men armed with light firelocks. In this year the King added a company of men armed with hand-grenades to each of the old British regiments, which was designated the "grenadier company." Daggers were so contrived as to fit in the muzzles of the muskets, and bayonets similar to those at present in use were adopted about twenty years afterwards.

An Ordnance regiment was raised in 1685, by order of King James II., to guard the artillery, and was designated the Royal Fusiliers (now 7th Foot). This corps, and the companies of grenadiers, did not carry pikes.

King William III. incorporated the Admiral's regiment in the second Foot Guards, and raised two Marine regiments for sea-service. During the war in this reign, each company of infantry (excepting the fusiliers and grenadiers) consisted of 14 pikemen and 46 musketeers; the captains carried pikes; lieutenants, partisans; ensigns, half-pikes; and serjeants, halberds. After the peace in 1697 the Marine regiments were disbanded, but were again formed on the breaking out of the war in 1702.*

During the reign of Queen Anne the pikes were laid aside, and every infantry soldier was armed with a musket, bayonet, and sword; the grenadiers ceased, about the same period, to carry hand grenades; and the regiments were directed to lay aside their third colour: the corps of Royal Artillery was first added to the Army in this reign.

About the year 1745, the men of the battalion companies of infantry ceased to carry swords; during

---

* The 30th, 31st, and 32nd Regiments were formed as Marine corps in 1702, and were employed as such during the wars in the reign of Queen Anne. The Marine corps were embarked in the Fleet under Admiral Sir George Rooke, and were at the taking of Gibraltar, and in its subsequent defence in 1704; they were afterwards employed at the siege of Barcelona in 1705.

the reign of George II. light companies were added to infantry regiments; and in 1764 a Board of General Officers recommended that the grenadiers should lay aside their swords, as that weapon had never been used during the seven years' war. Since that period the arms of the infantry soldier have been limited to the musket and bayonet.

The arms and equipment of the British troops have seldom differed materially, since the Conquest, from those of other European states; and in some respects the arming has, at certain periods, been allowed to be inferior to that of the nations with whom they have had to contend; yet, under this disadvantage, the bravery and superiority of the British infantry have been evinced on very many and most trying occasions, and splendid victories have been gained over very superior numbers.

Great Britain has produced a race of lion-like champions who have dared to confront a host of foes, and have proved themselves valiant with any arms. At *Crecy* King Edward III., at the head of about 30,000 men, defeated, on the 26th of August, 1346, Philip King of France, whose army is said to have amounted to 100,000 men; here British valour encountered veterans of renown:—the King of Bohemia, the King of Majorca, and many princes and nobles were slain, and the French army was routed and cut to pieces. Ten years afterwards, Edward Prince of Wales, who was designated the Black Prince, defeated, at *Poictiers*, with 14,000 men, a French army of 60,000 horse, besides infantry, and took John I., King of France, and his son

Philip, prisoners. On the 25th of October, 1415, King Henry V., with an army of about 13,000 men, although greatly exhausted by marches, privations, and sickness, defeated, at *Agincourt*, the Constable of France, at the head of the flower of the French nobility and an army said to amount to 60,000 men, and gained a complete victory.

During the seventy years' war between the United Provinces of the Netherlands and the Spanish monarchy, which commenced in 1578 and terminated in 1648, the British infantry in the service of the States-General were celebrated for their unconquerable spirit and firmness;* and in the thirty years' war between the Protestant Princes and the Emperor of Germany, the British troops in the service of Sweden and other states were celebrated for deeds of heroism.† In the wars of Queen Anne, the fame of the British army under the great MARLBOROUGH was spread throughout the world; and if we glance at the achievements performed within the memory of persons now living, there is abundant proof that the Britons of the present age are not inferior to their ancestors in the qualities

---

* The brave Sir Roger Williams, in his Discourse on War, printed in 1590, observes:—" I persuade myself ten thousand of our nation would beat thirty thousand of theirs (the Spaniards) out of the field, let them be chosen where they list." Yet at this time the Spanish infantry was allowed to be the best disciplined in Europe. For instances of valour displayed by the British Infantry during the Seventy Years' War, see the Historical Record of the Third Foot, or Buffs.

† Vide the Historical Record of the First, or Royal Regiment of Foot.

which constitute good soldiers. Witness the deeds of the brave men, of whom there are many now surviving, who fought in Egypt in 1801, under the brave Abercromby, and compelled the French army, which had been vainly styled *Invincible*, to evacuate that country; also the services of the gallant Troops during the arduous campaigns in the Peninsula, under the immortal WELLINGTON; and the determined stand made by the British Army at Waterloo, where Napoleon Bonaparte, who had long been the inveterate enemy of Great Britain, and had sought and planned her destruction by every means he could devise, was compelled to leave his vanquished legions to their fate, and to place himself at the disposal of the British Government. These achievements, with others of recent dates in the distant climes of India, prove that the same valour and constancy which glowed in the breasts of the heroes of Crecy, Poictiers, Agincourt, Blenheim, and Ramilies, continue to animate the Britons of the nineteenth century.

The British Soldier is distinguished for a robust and muscular frame,—intrepidity which no danger can appal,—unconquerable spirit and resolution,—patience in fatigue and privation, and cheerful obedience to his superiors. These qualities, united with an excellent system of order and discipline to regulate and give a skilful direction to the energies and adventurous spirit of the hero, and a wise selection of officers of superior talent to command, whose presence inspires confidence,—have been the leading causes of the splendid victories gained by the British arms.* The fame of the deeds of the past and present generations in the various battle-fields where the robust sons of Albion have fought and conquered, surrounds the British arms with a halo of glory; these achievements will live in the page of history to the end of time.

The records of the several regiments will be found to contain a detail of facts of an interesting character, connected with the hardships, sufferings, and gallant exploits of British soldiers in the various parts of the world, where the calls of their Country and the commands of their Sovereign have required them to proceed in the execution of their duty, whether in

---

* " Under the blessing of Divine Providence, His Majesty ascribes the successes which have attended the exertions of his troops in Egypt to that determined bravery which is inherent in Britons; but His Majesty desires it may be most solemnly and forcibly impressed on the consideration of every part of the army, that it has been a strict observance of order, discipline, and military system, which has given the full energy to the native valour of the troops, and has enabled them proudly to assert the superiority of the national military character, in situations uncommonly arduous, and under circumstances of peculiar difficulty."—*General Orders in* 1801.

In the General Orders issued by Lieut.-General Sir John Hope (afterwards Lord Hopetoun), congratulating the army upon the successful result of the Battle of Corunna, on the 16th of January, 1809, it is stated:—" On no occasion has the undaunted valour of British troops ever been more manifest. At the termination of a severe and harassing march, rendered necessary by the superiority which the enemy had acquired, and which had materially impaired the efficiency of the troops, many disadvantages were to be encountered. These have all been surmounted by the conduct of the troops themselves; and the enemy has been taught, that whatever advantages of position or of numbers he may possess, there is inherent in the British officers and soldiers a bravery that knows not how to yield,—that no circumstances can appal,—and that will ensure victory, when it is to be obtained by the exertion of any human means."

active continental operations, or in maintaining colonial territories in distant and unfavourable climes.

The superiority of the British infantry has been pre-eminently set forth in the wars of six centuries, and admitted by the greatest commanders which Europe has produced. The formations and movements of this *arme*, as at present practised, while they are adapted to every species of warfare, and to all probable situations and circumstances of service, are calculated to show forth the brilliancy of military tactics calculated upon mathematical and scientific principles. Although the movements and evolutions have been copied from the continental armies, yet various improvements have from time to time been introduced, to insure that simplicity and celerity by which the superiority of the national military character is maintained. The rank and influence which Great Britain has attained among the nations of the world, have in a great measure been purchased by the valour of the Army, and to persons who have the welfare of their country at heart, the records of the several regiments cannot fail to prove interesting.

SIXTEENTH REGIMENT OF FOOT.

CONTENTS

OF THE

HISTORICAL RECORD.

Year		Page
	INTRODUCTION	
1688	Formation of the Regiment	1
——	Establishment and Uniform	2
——	Quartered at Stony Stratford	–
1689	Embarked for Holland	3
——	Engaged at Walcourt	–
——	Marched to Bruges	4
1690	Marched to Brussels	–
1691	Joined the Army in South Brabant . . .	–
1692	Engaged at Steenkirk	–
——	Colonel Hodges killed	5
1693	Engaged at Landen	–
——	Quartered at Dendermond	–
1694	Joined the Army in the Field	6
——	Returned to Dendermond	–
1695	Joined in the Siege and Capture of Namur .	–
1696	Joined the Army of Brabant	–
1697	Treaty of Peace concluded at Ryswick . .	7
——	Embarked for Ireland	–
1701	Preparations for recommencing War with France	–
——	Re-embarked for Holland	–
——	Reviewed on Breda-Heath by King William III.	–

CONTENTS.

Year		Page
1702	Proceeded to Rosendael	7
—	Encamped at Cranenburg	—
—	Siege of Kayserswerth	—
—	Marched to Nimeguen	—
—	War declared against France	8
—	Earl of Marlborough assumed the command of the Army	—
—	Siege of Venloo	—
—	——— Ruremonde	—
—	——— Stevenswaert	—
—	Capture of the Citadel of Liege	—
—	Returned to Holland	—
1703	Marched towards Maestricht	—
—	Siege and Capture of Huy	—
—	——————————— Limburg	—
—	Returned to Holland	—
1704	Accompanied the Army to Germany	9
—	Battle of Schellenberg	—
—	Crossed the Danube	—
—	Battle of Blenheim	—
—	Marshal Tallard, and many officers and soldiers, made prisoners	—
—	Returned to Holland	10
1705	Attacks on Helixem and Neer-Hespen	—
1706	Battle of Ramilies	11
—	Surrender of principal towns of Brabant	—
—	Marched into quarters at Ghent	—
1708	Returned to England to repel invasion by the Pretender	—
—	Returned to Flanders	—
—	Proceeded to Ghent	—
—	Battle of Oudenarde	—
—	Siege of Lisle	12
—	Surrender of the Citadel of Lisle	—
1709	Siege and Capture of Tournay	13

CONTENTS. XXV

Year		Page
1709	Battle of Malplaquet	13
—	Siege and Surrender of Mons	14
—	Marched into winter-quarters at Ghent	—
1710	Engaged in forcing the French Lines at Pont-a-Vendin	—
—	Siege and Surrender of Douay	—
—	———————— Bethune	—
—	———————— Aire and St. Venant	—
—	Returned to Ghent	—
1711	Engaged in forcing the French Lines at Arleux	—
—	Siege of Bouchain	—
1712	Joined the Army at Tournay	15
—	Encamped at Cateau-Cambresis	—
—	Surrender of Quesnoy	—
—	Suspension of hostilities	—
—	Detached to Dunkirk	—
1714	Embarked for Scotland	—
1739	War declared against Spain	16
1740	Encamped near Newbury under Lieutenant-General Wade	17
—	Embarked as Marines	—
—	Re-landed at Portsmouth	—
—	A detachment embarked for the West Indies on an Expedition under General Lord Cathcart	—
1741	Expedition arrived at Jamaica	—
—	Employed at Carthagena, in South America	—
—	Detachment nearly annihilated by disease	—
1742	War of the Austrian Succession commenced	—
1745	Arrival in Scotland of Charles Edward, eldest son of the Pretender	—
1746	Regiment embarked for Scotland	18
1748	Termination of the War on the Continent	—
1749	Embarked for Ireland	—
1751	Royal Warrant issued on 1st July for regulating the Clothing, Colours, &c. of Regiments	—

YEAR		PAGE
1755	War re-commenced with France	19
1763	Peace of Fontainebleau took place	—
1767	Embarked for Florida in South America	20
1775	War commenced with North America	—
1778	War commenced with France, Spain, and Holland	21
1779	Regiment withdrew to Baton Rouge, and made prisoners of war by the Spanish Governor of Louisiana	—
——	Engaged with French and American forces at Savannah and the State of Georgia	—
1781	Defended Pensacola against a Spanish force	22
1782	Returned to England from South America	23
——	Authorized to assume the County Title of *Buckinghamshire* Regiment	—
——	Termination of the American War	—
1784	Embarked for Ireland	—
1790	Embarked for Nova Scotia	24
1791	Removed to Jamaica	—
1793	Revolution broke out in France	—
——	Republican principles extended to the French West India Settlements	—
——	Detachment embarked from Jamaica for St. Domingo	—
1795	Engaged in the Maroon War in Jamaica	—
1796	Maroons reduced to submission, and removed from Jamaica	25
——	Regiment returned to England	—
1797	Embarked for Scotland	—
1799	Returned to England	26
1800	Embarked for Ireland	—
1802	Peace of Amiens concluded	—
1803	War with France recommenced	—
1804	Embarked for the West Indies	—
——	Employed on an Expedition against Surinam	27

CONTENTS. xxvii

YEAR		PAGE
1806	Attacked by a large force of predatory Negroes at Surinam	27
1809	The County Title exchanged to the *Bedfordshire* instead of the Buckinghamshire Regiment .	28
1811	Returned to England	—
1813	Embarked for Scotland	—
——	Proceeded to Ireland	—
1814	War took place with the United States of America	29
——	Embarked for Canada	—
1815	Returned to England, proceeded to Ostend, and marched to Paris	—
——	Returned to England	—
1816	Embarked for Ireland	30
1819	Embarked for Ceylon	—
1828	Embarked for Bengal	31
1841	Embarked for England	32
1843	Proceeded to Ireland	33
1846	Six Service Companies embarked for Gibraltar	34
1847	Six Service Companies embarked for Corfu	—
1848	Four Depôt Companies embarked from Cork for Guernsey	—
——	The Conclusion	—

PLATES.

Costume of the Regiment . . . . to face	1
Colours of the Regiment . . . . ,,	34

SUCCESSION OF COLONELS

OF THE

SIXTEENTH REGIMENT OF FOOT.

Year		Page
1688	Archibald Douglas	35
——	Robert Hodges	36
1692	*Hon.* James Stanley, afterwards Earl of Derby.	—
1705	Francis Godfrey	37
1711	Henry Durell	38
1713	Hans Hamilton	—
1715	Richard *Viscount* Irwin	—
1717	James Cholmeley	39
1724	Henry Earl of Deloraine, K.B.	—
1730	Roger Handasyd	40
1763	*Hon.* Robert Brudenell	—
1765	Sir William Draper, K.B.	—
1766	James Gisborne	41
1778	James Robertson	—
1788	*Hon.* Thomas Bruce	42
1797	Henry Bowyer	—
1808	Sir Charles Green, Bart.	43
1814	Sir George Prevost, Bart.	44
1816	Hugh Mackay Gordon	45
1823	William Carr, *Viscount* Beresford, G.C.B. and G.C.H.	—

SIXTEENTH REGIMENT OF FOOT.

FOR CANNON'S MILITARY RECORDS

HISTORICAL RECORD

OF

THE SIXTEENTH,

OR THE

BEDFORDSHIRE REGIMENT OF FOOT.

In the autumn of 1688, when the pernicious counsellors of King James II. had induced His Majesty to adopt measures which indicated a design to overthrow the constitution and established religion of the country, and many patriotic noblemen and gentlemen had solicited the Prince of Orange to come to England with an army, to preserve the liberties and religion of the people, the King then became sensible of the dangerous position into which he had been brought, and resolved to augment his army: and among the corps embodied on that occasion was a regiment of pikemen and musketeers, which has been retained in the service to the present time, and now bears the title of " The SIXTEENTH, or the BEDFORDSHIRE Regiment of Foot."

This corps was raised in the southern counties of England, and the colonelcy was conferred on Lieut.-Colonel Archibald Douglas, from the royal regiment of foot, by commission dated the 9th of October, 1688. Captain Robert Hodges, from the grenadier company of the royal regiment, was appointed Lieut.-Colonel,

1688 and Murdock M'Kenzie was nominated Major. The establishment was fixed at nine hundred and twenty-seven officers and soldiers, including a grenadier company, which was afterwards ordered to be added to the regiment. The uniform was round hats, ornamented with *white* ribands; *red* coats, lined and faced with *white;* white waistcoats and breeches.

Five days after the warrants for the formation of the regiment were issued, a number of men had enrolled themselves under the standards of this corps,—principally from the county of Middlesex; and they were ordered to march to Reading in Berkshire, where the several enlisting parties were directed to assemble, and the formation of the corps was completed.

Early in November, when the armament under the Prince of Orange had passed Dover, the regiment was ordered to march to London, and occupy quarters in the borough of Southwark; it was afterwards directed to join the army: but the pernicious advice of the King's counsellors proved fatal to his interests; his soldiers refused to fight against the Prince of Orange; and some irregular orders were issued which appeared to leave the officers and men at liberty to quit their colours, when a number of corps were disbanded. The Prince of Orange issued orders for the several corps to be re-organised, and appointed quarters for every regiment;—the SIXTEENTH were directed to occupy quarters at Stony Stratford, in Buckinghamshire. King James afterwards fled to France.

Colonel Douglas adhered to the interest of King James, and the Prince of Orange promoted Lieut.-Colonel Hodges to the colonelcy of the regiment, by commission dated the 31st of December, 1688.

1689 In the early part of 1689 the Prince and Princess of

Orange were elevated to the throne by the titles of 1689
King William the Third and Queen Mary; and soon
afterwards the SIXTEENTH regiment received orders to
proceed to Holland, to aid the Dutch in their war
with France. It embarked for the United Provinces
in April, and served the campaign of that year under
Prince Waldeck; in August it was in position in the
province of Namur.

Early on the morning of the 25th of August, the
musketeers of the regiment, with the piquets of several
other corps, commanded by Colonel Hodges of the
SIXTEENTH, advanced to cover the numerous foraging
parties sent to the villages and fields in front of the
army, and Colonel Hodges posted his men at, and in
front of, the village of Forgé. About nine o'clock the
French army under Marshal d'Humières was seen
advancing to attack the confederate forces, when three
guns were fired to call in the foragers, and Colonel
Hodges prepared to resist the leading corps of the
enemy to give time for the several parties to withdraw.
The Dutch and Danish horse in front were speedily
driven in; but the musketeers of the SIXTEENTH and
other corps under Colonel Hodges lined the hedges,
and held a force of very superior numbers in check
nearly two hours, when, the foraging parties having
all returned to camp, Colonel Hodges withdrew to a
mill, and, posting his men behind walls and out-build-
ings, he held the French army in check nearly an hour,
the shots of his marksmen smiting the leading companies
of the enemy with sure aim. At length he received
orders to retire, and withdrew fighting, until he came
to the village of *Walcourt*, where a regiment of Lunen-
burgers was posted. The French attempted to carry
the village by storm; but were repulsed, and were

1689 eventually forced to retreat, with severe loss. Colonel Hodges' party had Lieut.-Colonel Graham, Captain Davison, and thirty men, killed.

In October the regiment marched to Bruges, where it was stationed during the winter.

1690 The regiment marched for Brussels in June, 1690, in order to join the Dutch forces; but Prince Waldeck engaged the French at Fleurus, without waiting for the arrival of the British troops, and his army was nearly annihilated; which reduced the confederate forces to the necessity of limiting their services to defensive operations during the remainder of the campaign.

1691 Leaving its winter quarters in March, 1691, the regiment joined the army in South Brabant, and was formed in brigade with the Scots foot guards, a battalion of the royals, and the Scots regiments of Ramsay, Angus, and Mackay; but the confederate army was not sufficiently numerous to prevent the French capturing Mons. During the summer the regiment took part in various manœuvres; but no general engagement occurred.

1692 In the spring of 1692, when the French besieged Namur, the SIXTEENTH were called from their winter quarters, and joined the army under the command of King William III., who advanced to relieve the besieged fortress, but was delayed by heavy rains, and the garrison surrendered before the end of June.

After several movements King William resolved to attack the French army, under Marshal Luxemburg, at its camp at *Steenkirk*, on the 3rd of August. The leading corps penetrated along difficult roads, and attacked the French army with great gallantry; but the main body of the confederate troops was too far in the rear to afford timely support, and the King ordered a retreat. The SIXTEENTH were brought into action on this occasion, and exposed to the enemy's fire, when Colonel Hodges was killed at the head of the regiment by a cannon-ball: his death was much regretted, he being a gallant and intelligent officer, much esteemed and beloved by the soldiers.

1692

King William conferred the colonelcy of the regiment on the Honorable James Stanley, afterwards Earl of Derby, from Captain and Lieut.-Colonel in the first foot guards.

Towards the end of August the regiment was detached, with other troops, under Lieut,-General Talmash, who moved towards Bruges: at the same time Furnes and Dixmude were taken possession of and fortified.

The regiment served the campaign of 1693 in the brigade commanded by Brigadier-General Erle. It took part in several movements, and was in position when the confederate army was attacked at *Landen,* on the 29th of July, by the French, under Marshal Luxemburg. The enemy had a great superiority of numbers on this occasion, and the confederate army was forced to retreat. It was stated in the London Gazette, "the enemy had above eighty thousand " effective men; we were not more than forty-five " thousand. * * * Our troops in general behaved " themselves extremely well, but the English did par- " ticularly distinguish themselves." The regiment had Captain Cole and Ensign Johnston killed, and Ensign Campion taken prisoner; it also lost upwards of fifty men, killed, wounded, and taken prisoners.

1693

At the end of the campaign the regiment was placed in garrison at Dendermond.

1694 Quitting its winter quarters in May, 1694, the regiment joined the army, and served the campaign of this year in the brigade commanded by Brigadier-General Collier: it afterwards returned to Dendermond.

1695 In 1695 King William undertook the siege of *Namur*, and the SIXTEENTH had the honor to take part in the capture of this important fortress. They joined the besieging army, and were on duty in the trenches on the 7th of July; and they were repeatedly engaged in storming the outworks and exterior defences. On the 17th of July Ensign Gardiner of the regiment was killed, and Ensign Devreux wounded, at the attack on the counterscarp; and on the 2nd of August, Captain Holiday of the grenadier company was wounded at the extending of the lodgment on the covered way. On the following day, when preparations were making for another assault, the garrison hoisted a white flag and agreed to surrender the town.

The SIXTEENTH were selected to take part in the siege of the castle of Namur, and were encamped at Maison Blanche; but, having lost many men, they were relieved on the 11th of August, and joined the covering army under the Prince of Vaudemont. They were encamped a short time between Genappe and Waterloo; afterwards near Namur; and the grenadier company took part in the attack on the castle, which capitulated on the 2nd of September. The regiment afterwards returned to Dendermond.

1696 Leaving its winter quarters in the spring of 1696, the regiment joined the army of Brabant under King William, and served the campaign of that year in Brigadier-General Fitzpatrick's brigade. It served the
1697 campaign of 1697 in the brigade under Brigadier-General Ingoldsby; and in the autumn the British

THE BEDFORDSHIRE REGIMENT OF FOOT. 7

monarch witnessed his efforts to preserve the reformed 1697
religion, and the balance of power in Europe, attended
with success. The treaty of Ryswick gave peace to the
nations of Europe; and the SIXTEENTH regiment embarked for Ireland, where it was stationed until the
summer of 1701, reposing on the reputation which it
had acquired on the continent, where it had served
seven campaigns.

In the meantime the French monarch had violated 1701
the liberties of Europe, by procuring the accession of
his grandson, the Duke of Anjou, to the throne of
Spain,—by seizing on the Spanish Netherlands and
detaining the Dutch garrisons in the barrier towns:
and the SIXTEENTH were called from their quarters in
Ireland to reinforce the Dutch army. The regiment
embarked from Carrickfergus on the 7th of June, and
sailed to the island of Voorn, where it was removed on
board of Dutch vessels, and proceeded up the Maese
to the fortress of Huesden, where it remained two
months, then proceeded to Breda, and was reviewed on
Breda heath by King William on the 21st of September, afterwards returning to Huesden.

In March, 1702, the regiment traversed the country 1702
to Rosendael, where the British corps were assembled
under Brigadier-General Ingoldsby, and received
information of the death of King William, and the
accession of Queen Anne, on the 8th of March. The
regiment afterwards marched across the country to the
duchy of Cleves, and encamped at Cranenburg,
forming part of the covering army during the siege of
Kayserswerth by the Germans. On the night of the
10th of June the covering army made a forced march
to *Nimeguen* to avoid the loss of communication
with that fortress, in consequence of the movements of

1702 the enemy. On the following morning the British corps in the rear-guard distinguished themselves in a sharp skirmish with the leading columns of the French army.

Queen Anne declared war against France; additional troops were sent to Holland, and the Earl of Marlborough assumed the command of the allied army. The SIXTEENTH shared in the operations by which the French army was forced to retire from the frontiers of Holland; and they formed part of the covering army during the sieges of *Venloo, Ruremonde,* and *Stevenswaert;* took part in delivering the city of *Liege* from the power of the enemy; and their grenadier company distinguished itself in the capture of the citadel by storm on the 23rd of October. The regiment afterwards marched back to Holland for winter quarters.

1703 Towards the end of April, 1703, the regiment commenced its march towards Maestricht, and was in position near that city when the French army approached in order of battle, but did not venture to hazard a general engagement. The regiment shared in the operations by which the French were afterwards forced to make a precipitate retreat and take post behind their fortified lines. The services of the regiment were also connected with the siege and capture of the fortress of *Huy,* on the Maese river, above the city of Liege; and with the siege of the city of *Limburg,* situate on a pleasant eminence among woods near the banks of the Wesdet, which place surrendered on the 28th of September. After these conquests the SIXTEENTH returned to Holland.

During the winter six hundred men of the regiment joined the garrison of Maestricht, while the Dutch soldiers were working at the entrenchments on the heights of Petersberg: in May, 1704, the remainder of the regiment marched towards the Rhine, and was joined at Bedburg by the detachment from Maestricht.

1704

The Duke of Marlborough led his army from Holland to the heart of Germany, and, there encountering the legions of France and Bavaria, he gained two important victories on the banks of the Danube, and exalted the reputation of the British arms. The SIXTEENTH had the honor to share in this splendid enterprise, and to take a distinguished part in gaining the victory at *Schellenberg* on the 2nd of July, when the regiment had Major Mordaunt, Ensign Charleston, one serjeant, and nineteen soldiers killed; Lieut.- Colonel Hamilton, Captain Coghlan, Ensign Key, one serjeant, and thirty-four rank and file wounded.

After this victory the regiment crossed the Danube and marched to the vicinity of the enemy's fortified camp at Augsburg, which was found too strong to be attacked, and the army retired a few stages, the Germans commencing the siege of Ingoldstadt. The enemy, being reinforced from France, took up a position in the valley of the Danube, near the village of *Blenheim*, which was occupied by a considerable body of troops; and on the memorable 13th of August a general engagement took place, in which the English general was once more victorious; the French and Bavarian army sustaining a decisive overthrow, with the loss of its artillery and baggage, and many entire regiments being made prisoners; the French commander, Marshal Tallard, being among the captives. The SIXTEENTH regiment was one of the corps which sustained the brunt of the battle on this occasion, and acquired great honor. The loss of the regiment was very great: Captain Coghlan, Lieutenant Brown, Ensigns Sabine and Hesketh, were among the killed;

1704 and Lieut.-Colonel Hamilton, Captains Hesketh, Fleming, Lee, and Horne, Lieutenants Vicariage, Jackson, Ayloffe, and Reddish,. Ensigns Mackrich, Hook, and Gordon, wounded.

From the banks of the Danube the regiment traversed the country to Philipsburg, where it crossed the Rhine, and formed part of the covering army encamped at Croon-Weissemberg, during the siege of *Landau* by the Germans. In the autumn the regiment embarked in boats on the Rhine, and sailed to Holland.

1705 The losses of the preceding campaigns were replaced in the spring of 1705 by recruits from England, and, when the regiment took the field to serve the campaign of 1705, its appearance and efficiency were admired. It was employed in the expedition up the Moselle, and, passing the Moselle and the Saar rivers on the 3rd of June, advanced towards Syrk; but the designs of the British commander were frustrated by the tardy movements of the Germans, and he marched back to the Netherlands.

In May of this year the Earl of Derby retired from the service, and was succeeded in the Colonelcy by Lieut.-Colonel Francis Godfrey, from the foot-guards.

A stupendous barrier of fortified lines, forts, and batteries opposed the progress of the British commander; but by skilful movements these works were passed at the slenderly-guarded posts of *Helixem* and *Neer-Hespen* on the 18th of July. On this occasion the SIXTEENTH formed part of Brigadier-General Fergusson's brigade in the main body of the army, and did not sustain any loss. It shared in the subsequent operations of the campaign, and passed the winter in garrison in Holland.

1706 The SIXTEENTH had the honor to take part in the

battle of *Ramilies*, on the 23rd of May, 1706, when the 1706 French, Spanish, and Bavarian forces, commanded by Marshal Villeroy and the Elector of Bavaria, were forced from their formidable position with severe loss, and pursued many miles.

Important results followed this triumph over the forces of Louis XIV.; the states of Brabant and magistrates of Brussels renounced their allegiance to the Duke of Anjou; the principal towns of Brabant and several fortified places in Flanders were immediately delivered up, and others surrendered after short sieges. Thus provinces disputed for ages, and towns which had resisted powerful armies for months and years, were conquered in one campaign. After taking part in these splendid achievements, the SIXTEENTH marched into quarters at Ghent.

The regiment was in the field during the campaign 1707 of 1707; but the French avoided an engagement, and nothing of importance occurred.

In the spring of 1708 the King of France fitted out a 1708 fleet, and prepared a land force for the invasion of Great Britain in favour of the Pretender, and the SIXTEENTH were ordered to return to England to repel the invaders: they arrived at Tynemouth on the 21st of March; but the French fleet having been chased from the British coast by the English navy, the regiment returned to Flanders.

After remaining a few weeks at Ghent, the regiment joined the army in the field, and took part in achieving another victory over the armies of Louis XIV., in the fields near *Oudenarde*, on the 11th of July. The SIXTEENTH formed part of a division of twenty battalions commanded by the Duke of Argyle, which traversed the Scheldt by the pontoon bridge between Oudenarde and the abbey of Eename, ascended the

1708 heights of Bevere, and, inclining to the right, engaged the enemy in the open grounds beyond the rivulet; when a fierce conflict of musketry ensued, and the French were driven from field to field, with great slaughter, until the darkness of the night rendered it impossible to distinguish friends from foes, when the troops were directed to cease firing. The wreck of the French army made a precipitate retreat.

The siege of the important fortress of *Lisle* was afterwards undertaken, and the SIXTEENTH were selected to take part in this gigantic enterprise, which excited universal attention throughout Europe; the strength of the place,—the garrison consisting of fifteen thousand men under the celebrated Marshal Boufflers, and being provided with everything necessary for a protracted defence,—gave an interesting character to this undertaking.

When the besieging army appeared before Lisle, the French out-guards retired, and *Serjeant Littler* of the SIXTEENTH regiment swam across the river with a hatchet, and cut the fastenings which held up a drawbridge to enable a party to pass the stream, for which act of gallantry he was rewarded with a commission in the third foot, or the Buffs.

The SIXTEENTH regiment took its turn of duty in the trenches and shared in the attacks during the siege of Lisle, evincing, on all occasions, the same heroic gallantry for which it had previously been distinguished. It had one serjeant and eleven rank and file killed, and four serjeants and fifty rank and file wounded, at the storming of the counterscarp; and sustained severe loss on several other occasions. Numerous difficulties had to be overcome in carrying on this siege; but the skill, valour, and perseverance of the officers and soldiers of the allied army, overcame every obstacle, and on the 9th of December the citadel surrendered. 1708

After reposing a few weeks in quarters, and receiving a draft of recruits from England, the regiment advanced up the country, and was encamped with the army on the Upper Dyle; it was subsequently employed in covering the siege of *Tournay*, and after the surrender of the town, on the 29th of July, 1708, the SIXTEENTH were selected to take part in the siege of the citadel. This proved a difficult service, in consequence of the extensive subterraneous works by which the fortress was surrounded. The approaches were carried on underground, and the working parties frequently penetrated the subterraneous labyrinths of the castle, and, encountering detachments of the enemy, fought underground with sword, pistol, and bayonet. Several parties were destroyed by the mines; but the works were persevered in, and the garrison surrendered in the beginning of September. 1709

After the capture of Tournay the army marched towards Mons; but finding a numerous French force, under Marshals Villars and Boufflers, in position at *Malplaquet*, the enemy was attacked in his fortified post on the morning of the 11th of September, and the SIXTEENTH had the honor to contribute to the gaining of another victory over the armies of France. On this occasion, the regiment was formed in brigade with the Buffs and the regiments of Temple and Evans (afterwards disbanded), and was engaged in the attack of the woods in which the enemy's left wing was posted, and in its advance it encountered entrenchments and breastworks bristling with bayonets, and emitting a storm of musket-shot and cannon-balls, which thinned the British ranks. The leading corps were repulsed; but, fresh troops arriving, a general attack was made

1709 with so much resolution that the French were driven from their entrenchments into the wood, where a sharp fire of musketry was kept up, and the SIXTEENTH were engaged among the trees. Finally the French were overpowered at every part of the field, and forced to retreat.

The regiment had about fifty men killed and wounded; and Captain Ayloffe, Lieutenants Macrath, Whiting, and Lawder wounded. It was afterwards employed in covering the siege of *Mons*, and passed the winter in quarters at Ghent.

1710 Having received another draft of recruits, the regiment marched in April, 1710, to the vicinity of Tournay, where the army was directed to assemble; its services were connected with the forcing of the enemy's fortified lines at *Pont-à-Vendin;* it also formed part of the covering army during the siege of *Douay*, which fortress surrendered on the 27th of June. The regiment was afterwards employed in covering the siege of *Bethune,* and this fortress was captured before the end of August. The French army avoiding a general engagement, the fortresses of *Aire* and *St. Venant* were besieged at the same time, and after the capture of these towns, the regiment returned to Ghent.

1711 Brigadier-General Godfrey withdrew from the service, and was succeeded in the colonelcy of the regiment by Brigadier-General Henry Durell, from the foot guards, by commission dated the 17th of February, 1711.

In the campaign of this year the regiment shared in the operations by which the boasted impregnable lines, prepared by the French to arrest the progress of the allied armies, were passed at *Arleux*, on the 5th of August, and it was subsequently engaged in the siege of the strong fortress of *Bouchain*,—services which called forth all the powers of the active mind of the Duke of Marlborough, who proved himself superior to the French generals in all the qualities which constitute a great commander. Bouchain having been captured, the regiment was placed in garrison for the winter.

Once more taking the field in April, 1712, the regiment joined the army near Tournay, from whence it marched to the vicinity of Bouchain, and was encamped at Cateau-Cambresis during the siege of *Quesnoy* by the Germans; it brought six hundred and eighty-one rank and file into the field. The garrison of *Quesnoy* surrendered on the 4th of July; and soon afterwards a suspension of arms was proclaimed preparatory to a treaty of peace, and the British troops withdrew to the vicinity of Ghent, from whence the SIXTEENTH were detached to Dunkirk, which city the French monarch delivered into the hands of the British, as a pledge of his sincerity in the negotiations for peace.

On the 1st of December, 1712, Brigadier-General Durell died, and Queen Anne conferred the colonelcy of the regiment on Brigadier-General Hans Hamilton, from the thirty-fourth regiment, by commission dated the 23rd of June, 1713.

The regiment was stationed at Dunkirk until April, 1714, when it embarked for Scotland, and, landing at Leith, relieved the twenty-fifth regiment, which was ordered to embark for Ireland. The SIXTEENTH were stationed at Stirling in September, 1714, with the Inniskilling dragoons, when the arrival in London of King George I. from Hanover, was celebrated with public rejoicings.

In the summer of 1715 the colonelcy of the regiment was conferred on the Lieut.-Colonel, Richard

1715 Viscount Irving, in succession to Brigadier-General Hamilton.

A rebellion in favour of the Pretender broke out in Scotland in the autumn of this year, and the Earl of Mar headed the insurgent clans; but the SIXTEENTH did not take the field: the protection of Fort William was entrusted to their charge; and they were in gar-
1716 rison at this place in the early part of 1716, when the rebellion was suppressed by the troops under the Duke of Argyle.

1717 In December, 1717, Viscount Irving was removed to the second horse, now first dragoon guards, and was succeeded by Lieut.-Colonel John Cholmeley; and this
1724 officer dying in April, 1724, King George I. conferred the colonelcy on Henry Earl of Deloraine (son of James Duke of Monmouth), from the Scots troop of horse-grenadier-guards.

1725 The regiment was employed on home service in Great Britain during the whole of the reign of King George I.; it was one of the corps selected to proceed to
1727 Holland in 1727, to assist the Dutch in their war with the Imperialists; but no embarkation took place.

1730 On the 9th of July, 1730, the Earl of Deloraine was removed to the seventh horse, now sixth dragoon-guards, and the colonelcy of the regiment was conferred by King George II. on Colonel Roger Handasyd, from the twenty-second regiment.

1737 In 1737 the British merchants complained of the depredations committed on their vessels by the Spaniards in South America. A Convention was entered into between the two Crowns, which was, however, violated by the Spaniards in many instances.

1739 On the 23rd of October, 1739, a declaration of war against Spain was proclaimed, when the establishment of the regiment was augmented.

In the summer of 1740 the regiment pitched its 1740 tents near Newbury, where an encampment was formed of two regiments of horse, three of dragoons, and four of infantry, under Lieut.-General Wade. The SIXTEENTH left the camp and embarked on board the fleet, where they served as Marines a short time, and afterwards landed at Portsmouth. In the autumn they furnished a detachment to accompany the expedition to the West Indies, under General Lord Cathcart, who died on the passage.

The expedition arrived at Jamaica in January, 1741, 1741 and the detachment of the SIXTEENTH was employed in the attempt on *Carthagena*, the capital of an extensive and wealthy province in the country of Terra Firma, in South America. The violent periodical rains occurred before the conquest was achieved, and the armament proved of insufficient strength to capture the place; the country became deluged with water, the health of the soldiers was seriously impaired, and the enterprise was abandoned. The detachment of the SIXTEENTH was nearly annihilated by disease.

In this year the war of the Austrian succession 1742 commenced; and in 1742 a British army proceeded to Flanders to support the interests of the Archduchess, Maria Theresa; but the SIXTEENTH were employed on home service.

Charles Edward, eldest son of the Pretender, arrived 1745 in Scotland in the summer of 1745, and being joined by a number of the Highland clans, he made a desperate effort to overthrow the existing government, and to procure the accession of his father to the throne. At first some partial successes were gained by the insurgents; but the British nation evinced firmness and decision in supporting the rights of their sovereign, and

c

1745 in preserving the constitutional privileges of the people The services of the regiment were, at this period, limited to the south of England, where a body of troops was held in readiness to repel a menaced invasion by the French.

1746 In January, 1746, the royal troops, under Lieut.-General Hawley, were defeated by the Clans, on Falkirk moor, and additional forces were ordered to proceed to Scotland. In March the SIXTEENTH regiment embarked from Gravesend, with several other corps, for Edinburgh, and arrived at Leith as the guns of Edinburgh castle were firing for the decisive victory gained over the clans at Culloden. The regiment waited a few days on board the transports, until the return of an express from the army, when it received orders to sail northwards, and landed at the royal burgh of Nairn on the 1st of May. It was subsequently stationed at Elgin, &c.

1747 The regiment remained in Scotland, and in the summer of 1747 it was encamped in a valley environed by lofty mountains, near Fort Augustus.

1748 The war on the Continent terminated in 1748; and
1749 in the following year the regiment was reduced in numbers to the peace establishment, and sent to Ireland, where it was stationed nearly twenty years.

1751 On the 1st of July, 1751, King George II. issued a warrant for establishing uniformity in the clothing, standards, and colours of the several regiments of the regular army; and in this warrant the uniform of the SIXTEENTH, or Lieut.-General Roger Handasyd's regiment, was directed to be red, faced with *yellow*.* The

---

* The date when the facings were changed from white to yellow has not been ascertained.

first, or the King's colour, to be the great Union: the second, or regimental colour, to be of yellow silk, with the Union in the upper canton; in the centre of the colours, the rank of the regiment, in gold Roman characters, within a wreath of roses and thistles on the same stalk.

1751

At this period the soldiers of the regiment wore three-cornered cocked hats, bound with white lace, and ornamented with a white loop and a black cockade; red waistcoats; red breeches; white gaiters reaching above the knee, and fastened below the knee with a black garter; and white cravats; they also wore buff cross-belts.

The undetermined extent of the British territory in North America gave rise to hostilities with France in 1755, and the establishment of the army was considerably augmented in that and the two following years. Several expeditions were also fitted out; but the SIXTEENTH regiment was detained on home service in Ireland. In 1760 a plan was formed for attacking the French island of Belleisle, and the SIXTEENTH, mustering seven hundred men, under Lieut.-Colonel Gabbet, embarked on board of the fleet; but the enterprise was laid aside in consequence of the death of King George II., and the regiment returned to Ireland.

1755
1756
1757
1758
1760

On the termination of the war in 1762, the regiment was again reduced to the peace establishment.

1762

General Roger Handasyd died in January, 1763, and in June King George III. conferred the colonelcy of the regiment on the Honorable Robert Brudenell, third son of George Earl of Cardigan, from captain and lieut.-colonel in the third foot guards.

1763

In 1765 Colonel Brudenell was removed to the Fourth regiment of foot, and was succeeded in the

1765

1765 colonelcy of the SIXTEENTH, by Colonel William Draper, who had commanded one of the regiments raised in 1757, and numbered the Seventy-ninth regiment, which was disbanded in 1763.

1766 Colonel Draper was honoured with the dignity of a Knight of the Bath, and in 1766 he exchanged to the colonelcy of one of the corps disbanded in 1763 (the 121st regiment) with Colonel James Gisborne, who was performing the duty of Quartermaster-General in Ireland.

1767 The regiment embarked from Ireland in 1767, for North America, and was stationed in the pleasant and fertile territory of Florida, which had been ceded to Great Britain, by the Spaniards, in 1763, in exchange for the Havannah.

1768 The head-quarters were established at Pensacola,— a town of West Florida, situate at the head of a delightful bay, or basin, in the Gulf of Mexico; and the regiment furnished various detachments to occupy military stations in East and West Florida.

1775 In these pleasant and healthy quarters the regiment was stationed when a number of the British colonies in North America revolted, and declared themselves a free and independent people, under the title of the United States. This occurred in 1775, and in the following

1776 year the SIXTEENTH were withdrawn from Florida, to join the army at New York, under Lieut.-General Sir William Howe; but the necessity of having a small force in the ceded Spanish province was evident, and the SIXTEENTH having, during their residence of eight years in East and West Florida, acquired the confidence of the inhabitants and a knowledge of the country,

1777 and of the habits and language of the people, the regiment received orders to return to Pensacola, and other stations in East and West Florida, and on the confines of Georgia.

1777

Lieut.-General Gisborne died on the 20th of February, 1778, and King George III. conferred the colonelcy on Major-General James Robertson, from Colonel Commandant of the second battalion of the Sixtieth, who had previously performed the duties of Lieut.-Colonel of the SIXTEENTH regiment, many years, with reputation.

1778

Had the British revolted provinces been left unaided by European states, they would, doubtless, have been reduced to submission; but in 1778 the French monarch sent a numerous fleet and an army to their assistance; and in 1779 the court of Spain commenced hostilities against Great Britain, and this example was followed by the Dutch.

1778

1779

Don Bernard de Galvez, governor of the Spanish province of Louisiana, assembled a numerous force, and suddenly invaded the British territories on the banks of the Mississippi; and Lieut.-Colonel Dickson, of the SIXTEENTH, who commanded the troops in that district, being unable to oppose the invading army, withdrew to *Baton Rouge*, where he caused a redoubt to be constructed, which was scarcely completed when the Spanish army advanced in force against this post, which was invested on the 12th of September. On the 21st the enemy opened a battery of heavy cannon against the works, which were so much damaged in a few hours, that Colonel Dickson was obliged to surrender. The garrison, consisting of a detachment of the SIXTEENTH, Sixtieth, and of the Waldeck regiments, was sent prisoners of war to New Orleans, and afterwards exchanged.

The French armament, under the Comte d'Estaing, approached the city and port of *Savannah* in Chatham

1779 county, in the state of Georgia, early in September, and a detachment of the SIXTEENTH regiment, commanded by Major Graham, formed part of the force under Major-General Prevost, which defended that place. The French troops landed, and were joined by an American force under General Lincoln; but they encountered a resistance which proved the determined valour of the garrison. A detachment from the SIXTEENTH was engaged in a sally on the 24th of September, under Major Graham of the regiment, and this service was performed with judgment and bravery. " Major Graham artfully drew the enemy into a snare, " by which the French and Americans fired on each " other, and had fifty men killed before the mistake " was discovered."* Before daylight on the 9th of October, the French and Americans made a desperate effort to capture the place by storm ; but were repulsed at every point with severe loss. They afterwards raised the siege and retired.

1781 In 1781 the Spaniards sent a numerous sea and land force against Florida, under Don Bernard de Galvez, and the invading army commenced operations by an attack upon the works defending *Pensacola*, where a detachment of the SIXTEENTH regiment was stationed. From the strength of the Spanish force, mustering nine thousand men, and a numerous fleet, at the same time the British garrison only amounted to twelve hundred men, the reduction of the place appeared inevitable ; yet a gallant defence was made, and the soldiers displayed that innate bravery and resolution for which British troops have always been distinguished. On the morning of the 8th of May a shell burst near the door of the magazine of the advanced redoubt, set fire to the

---

* Beatson's Naval and Military Memoirs.

powder, and the redoubt and its garrison were destroyed 1781
by the explosion, excepting a few men, who were forced
to retire, after spiking the guns. The Spaniards
carried the redoubt, and threatened to storm the
remaining works; but were intimidated by the determined bearing of the garrison. The British commander, Major-General John Campbell, afterwards
agreed to surrender, on condition that the garrison
should march out with the honours of war, and be sent
to a part belonging to Great Britain, but not serve
against the Spaniards, or their allies, until exchanged.
The SIXTEENTH had Lieutenant Edward Carroll and
seven soldiers killed; Captain Anthony Foster and
five soldiers wounded. Pensacola was a flourishing
place while under the British; but it declined after it
was taken by the Spaniards.

The regiment having sustained severe loss from 1782
various services in Florida, Georgia, and South Carolina, where detachments had been employed, it was
ordered to return to Europe, and arrived in England in
March, 1782.

In August the regiment received directions to assume
the title of the SIXTEENTH, OR THE BUCKINGHAM Regiment, and to cultivate a connection with the respectable
inhabitants of that county, which might be useful
towards recruiting the regiment.

The American War terminated in 1782; and the regiment was placed upon a peace establishment in 1783.

In 1784 it embarked for Ireland, where it was sta- 1784
tioned several years under the orders of Lieut.-Colonel
James Henry Craig, an officer of great zeal and ability.

Lieut.-General Robertson, died on the 4th of March, 1788
1788, and was succeeded in the colonelcy by Major-
General the Honorable Thomas Bruce, from the late

1788 100th regiment, which was reduced after the termination of the American War.

1790 On the 18th of August, 1790, the regiment embarked
1791 from Ireland for Nova Scotia, and in 1791 it was removed to the island of Jamaica, where it remained five years.

1793 A revolution broke out in France, and the republican principles which filled that kingdom with anarchy, confusion, and bloodshed, soon extended to the French West India Settlements, where the blacks and mulattoes rose in arms against the European planters, and filled the islands with rapine and devastation. Many of the respectable inhabitants of the French island of *St. Domingo* solicited the protection of the British government against the fury of the blacks, and a detachment of British troops proceeded to their aid, from Jamaica, in 1793. The SIXTEENTH regiment furnished a portion of this detachment, but the climate of St. Domingo proved injurious to the health of the British troops,
1794 and the whole of the party of the SIXTEENTH died of a pestilential fever, excepting Lieutenant Vernon and one serjeant, who rejoined the regiment at Jamaica.

1795 The island of Jamaica was taken from the Spaniards, by an English armament in 1655 (during the commonwealth under Cromwell), when the slaves belonging to the Spanish planters fled to the mountains, where they lived in savage independence, and were called "Maroons." They procured arms, became expert marksmen, and frequently committed outrages against the British inhabitants. In 1738 a treaty was concluded with them, and they received a grant of land; but the pernicious doctrines of the French republicans were circulated among the Maroons, who were joined by a number of runaway slaves, and commenced hos-

THE BEDFORDSHIRE REGIMENT OF FOOT. 25

tilities against the English in 1795. The SIXTEENTH served in the *Maroon war*, when the soldiers encountered many difficulties, and at first sustained some reverses, from the difficult nature of the mountainous districts into which they had to penetrate, and from the expert character of the Maroon warriors in bush-fighting among rocks and dells covered with trees and underwood. A detachment of the SIXTEENTH was first called into action; and in October the regiment, commanded by Major John Skinner, who held the local rank of Colonel, was called into the field. This officer had served many years in the regiment; he had distinguished himself in the American war, while serving with Tarleton's Legion, with which corps he was present at numerous engagements, and on joining the field force in the Maroon war, his presence inspired the troops with confidence. Offensive operations were conducted with prudence and skill, and by a strict combination in the movements of the troops employed, united with valour and discipline, the Maroons were driven from their mountain-fastnesses, and chased from post to post, until they were forced to submit. In performing this service, the soldiers underwent great fatigue and privation, and they conquered the Maroons in a part of the island where no European had ever before thought of penetrating. Captain Drummond, of the SIXTEENTH, distinguished himself in this war.

The Maroons tendered their submission in March, 1796, and they were afterwards removed from the island.

Having become considerably reduced in numbers, the regiment returned to England, towards the close of this year, and was stationed a short time at Greenwich, from whence it embarked for Scotland, early in 1797; at the same time it was ordered to recruit with boys.

Lieut.-General the Honorable Thomas Bruce having

26 HISTORICAL RECORD OF THE SIXTEENTH, OR

1797 died, he was succeeded in the colonelcy by Major-General Henry Bowyer, from the Eighty-ninth regiment, by commission dated the 15th of December, 1797.

1798 The regiment was quartered in Fifeshire, under the orders of Major John Skinner, and afterwards proceeded to Fort George; Lieut.-Colonel Hugh Wallace assuming the command. The boys were transferred to the Thirty-fourth and Sixty-fifth regiments, under orders for India, and the SIXTEENTH were completed by volunteers from the English militia, principally limited service men.

1799 In 1799 the regiment embarked from Scotland for London, from whence it proceeded to Margate, to join the expedition to Holland, under His Royal Highness the Duke of York; but the order to proceed on this service was countermanded, and the regiment was stationed a few months at Horsham in Sussex.

1800 Embarking from Portsmouth in 1800, the regiment sailed to Cork, and was stationed in the south of Ireland; where Lieut.-Colonel St. John Fancourt
1801 joined and assume the command in 1801.

1802 At the conclusion of the peace of Amiens in 1802, the limited service men were discharged; and the regiment was completed from disbanded fencible and militia corps.

1803 War was resumed in 1803; and Lieut.-Colonel Fancourt having been removed to the Thirty-fourth regiment, the command of the SIXTEENTH devolved on Brevet Lieut.-Colonel Skinner.

1804 On the 7th of January, 1804, the regiment embarked from Monkstown, for the West Indies, and arrived at Barbadoes on the 26th of March. It was immediately ordered to hold itself in readiness to proceed with the expedition under Major-General Sir Charles Green and Commodore Samuel Hood, against the Dutch colony of

THE BEDFORDSHIRE REGIMENT OF FOOT. 27

Surinam, in Guiana, in South America. This colony was 1804 ceded to the Dutch, by King Charles II., in exchange for New York, in North America; it was captured by the British in 1799, and restored at the peace of Amiens in 1802.

On the 7th of April, 1804, the expedition sailed from Barbadoes, and a landing was effected on the 26th of that month; the SIXTEENTH were actively employed in operations, until the surrender of the colony on the 4th of May.

While the regiment was at Surinam, the post oc- 1806 cupied by a detachment of the light company and a few men of the fourth West India regiment, commanded by Lieutenant Richard Greene, of the SIXTEENTH, at *Armena*, was attacked by a large force of predatory negroes and banditti, and defended with great gallantry, the greater part of the garrison being killed in the successful resistance made to the assailants. The inhabitants of the colony afterwards presented Lieutenant Greene with a valuable sword, in token of their sense of his conduct.

In 1807 Lieut.-Colonel Skinner was succeeded in 1807 the duties of commanding officer by Major Brabazon Dean Vernon.*

---

* Lieutenant-General John Skinner entered the army as an Ensign in the SIXTEENTH regiment of foot on the 4th of September, 1772, and rose to the rank of Lieut.-Colonel of that regiment on the 11th of April, 1805: he was promoted to the rank of Colonel in the army on the 25th of April, 1808: after performing the duties of a regimental officer, in the various situations of service, from 1772, to 1811, he was advanced to the rank of Major-General on the 4th of June, 1811, and was appointed to the staff of the army in the West Indies, on which he continued to serve until the 24th of March, 1816: he was promoted to the rank of Lieut.-General on the 19th of July, 1821: he died in 1827, after a continued and faithful service of forty-four years.

1808 On the decease of General Bowyer, in 1808, King George III. conferred the colonelcy on Major-General Sir Charles Green, Bart., from the York light infantry volunteers.

1809 In May, 1809, His Majesty was graciously pleased to approve of the regiment being styled the SIXTEENTH, or the BEDFORDSHIRE, instead of the *Buckinghamshire*, Regiment: this exchange of County titles took place with the Fourteenth Regiment of Foot.

1810 Lieut.-Colonel Henry Tolley assumed the command of the regiment, in June, 1810.

During its stay at Surinam and Barbadoes, the regiment lost twenty-seven officers and upwards of five hundred men by disease. The survivors returned to
1811 England by detachments in 1810, 1811, and 1812, and
1812 landed at Falmouth and Portsmouth. One ship, the "Islam," having on board the remainder of the grenadiers and of one battalion company, was wrecked on the Tuscan Rock off the coast of Ireland. By the exertions of some workmen, who were making preparations to erect a lighthouse on the rock, all were saved excepting one man, one woman, and some children; all the arms, appointments, and baggage were lost. On the following day the party was taken off the rock by a brig, and conveyed to Beaumaris in Wales.

After occupying quarters at various stations, and receiving many volunteers from the English and Irish militia, the regiment marched to Sunderland in July;
1813 and in March, 1813, embarked from thence for Perth: in July of this year it proceeded to Ireland.

1814 Sir Charles Green, Baronet, was removed to the Thirty-seventh regiment in February, 1814, when His Royal Highness the Prince Regent, conferred the colonelcy of the SIXTEENTH on Lieut.-General Sir George Prevost, from the Seventy sixth regiment.

During this period the war was continued in Europe, 1814 and British troops were acquiring laurels under the Duke of Wellington: at the same time the measures pursued to counteract the decrees made by Napoleon, Emperor of the French, for the destruction of the commerce of Great Britain, brought on a war between the British Crown and the United States of North America; and in the spring of this year the SIXTEENTH embarked from Monkstown to join the British troops in Canada. The regiment was commanded by Colonel Tolley, and arriving at Quebec on the 29th of May, was stationed a short period at that fortress; it was afterwards removed to Chambly, from whence it proceeded to Montreal. The British troops having failed in the attack of the American post at Plattsburg, the SIXTEENTH were relieved from duty at Montreal, sent to the upper province, and stationed at Fort Wellington.

A treaty of peace having been concluded with the 1815 Americans, the regiment was ordered to return to Europe; it sailed from Quebec in July, and arrived at Portsmouth in August. The return of Buonaparte to France,—his reassumption of the imperial dignity,—his overthrow at Waterloo, and surrender to a British man-of-war, had occurred while the regiment was in Canada, and on the passage to Europe; on its arrival at Portsmouth, it was ordered to proceed to the Continent, to join the army commanded by the Duke of Wellington. The regiment landed at Ostend, and marching to Paris, encamped at St. Denis.

On the conclusion of the definitive treaties of peace, the regiment marched to Calais, where it embarked for England, and landing at Dover, remained there fourteen days.

Lieut.-General Sir George Prevost, Baronet, having 1816

1816 died, the Prince Regent nominated Major-General Hugh Mackay Gordon to the colonelcy of the regiment, from the York Chasseurs, by commission dated the 8th of January, 1816.

From Dover the regiment embarked for Ireland; it landed at Monkstown on the 3rd of February, and was stationed successively at Fermoy, Limerick, and Cashel.

1817 In 1817 the regiment was removed to Kilkenny;
1818 and in 1818 to Athlone.
1819 On the 25th of August, 1819, the regiment embarked from Cork, under the command of Colonel Tolley, for colonial service, and touching at the Cape of Good Hope, the flank companies landed, and remained at Cape Town a month. The battalion companies continued their voyage to Ceylon, and landed at Colombo
1820 on the 20th of February, 1820, under Major William Vandeleur. The flank companies, under Colonel Tolley, arrived in March.
1821 The regiment remained seventeen months at Colombo, where it was joined by one hundred and twenty-eight volunteers from the Seventy-third; in August, 1821, it marched, under Major Vandeleur, for Kandy, where Colonel Tolley resumed the command, and on his
1822 proceeding on leave of absence, in October, 1822, the command devolved on Brevet Lieut.-Colonel Lionel Hook.
1823 Lieut.-General Gordon died in the spring of 1823, and was succeeded in the colonelcy by Lieut.-General William Carr, Viscount Beresford, G.C.B., and G.C.H.
1824 In March, 1824, the regiment returned to Colombo, where it lost several officers and a number of men by a malignant fever.
1825 Colonel Tolley was promoted to the rank of Major-General; Brevet Lieut.-Colonel Hook was nominated

to a Lieut.-Colonelcy in the Ceylon rifle corps; and 1825
Colonel David Ximenes was appointed Lieut.-Colonel
of the SIXTEENTH; this officer arrived at Colombo in
March, 1826, and assumed the command of the 1826
regiment, which marched from Colombo, in July following, for Point de Galle.

On the 2nd of July, 1827, Lieutenants Alexander, 1827
Mylius, and Hyde, Ensigns Cassidi and Hannagan,
three serjeants, and one hundred and eight rank and
file, joined from the depôt in England.

The regiment, having been appointed to proceed to 1828
Bengal, was relieved from duty at the island of Ceylon,
by the Sixty-first, in November, 1828, and embarking
from thence in four divisions, arrived at Calcutta in
January, 1829, when Colonel Ximenes was appointed 1829
to command the garrison of Fort William, and Major
John W. Adain assumed the command of the regiment;
which received one hundred and fourteen volunteers
from the Fifty-ninth, and forty-six from the Thirtieth
and Forty-seventh regiments. In April Major Adain
obtained leave to proceed to England, and the command
of the regiment devolved on Major Adam Gordon
Campbell, until the arrival of Lieut.-Colonel Lionel
Smith Hook, in November: this officer was appointed
to the regiment in February of this year.

The SIXTEENTH remained on duty at Calcutta, where, 1830
in October and November, 1830, they received sixty-four volunteers from other corps.

In January, 1831, Colonel Hook was nominated to 1831
the command of the garrison of Fort William, and
Major Campbell resumed the command; but on the
regiment quitting Calcutta, in March following, to
proceed in steam-boats to Chinsurah, Colonel Hook
again assumed the command. At this period twenty
volunteers joined from the Royal regiment.

1832 The SIXTEENTH regiment remained at Chinsurha
1833 until December, 1833, when it commenced its march for Ghazepore: while on the march its destination was altered for Cawnpore; and on the 7th of February,
1834 1834, it had the misfortune to lose its commanding officer, Colonel Hook, who died at the camp at Secrole, Benares, when the command again devolved on Major Campbell: on the 28th of February the regiment arrived at Cawnpore.
1835 In March, 1835, Captain H. McManus, Ensigns Henry A. O'Molony and Edward Brabazon, two serjeants and forty-three rank and file, joined from England. Another detachment joined in May; and in March,
1836 1836, one hundred and six volunteers were received from the Thirty-eighth regiment,—also eighty-four recruits from England, under Captain R. Brown, Ensigns Hook and Lawson, and Surgeon Steele. They were followed by Ensigns G. M. Ross and H. C. M. Ximenes, in September.
1837 In March, 1837, Lieutenant Gibbs, and thirty-two recruits joined; and in May, twenty-two volunteers
1838 from the Twentieth regiment. Thirty-nine volunteers also joined from the Forty-fifth, in April, 1838.
1839 On the 24th of December, 1839, the regiment received orders to proceed by water to Calcutta; but in January,
1840 1840, it received orders to disembark at Dinapore, and relieve the Forty-ninth regiment, under orders to proceed with the expedition to China. The SIXTEENTH remained at Dinapore until October, when they were relieved by a wing of the Twenty-first fusiliers, and embarked for the Presidency, where they arrived on the 4th of November.

Orders having been issued for the regiment to return to England, it transferred a number of volunteers to other corps, and embarked, in three divisions, in

THE BEDFORDSHIRE REGIMENT OF FOOT. 33

December, 1840, and January, 1841, under Lieut.- 1841
Colonel Campbell, Major H. Clements, and Brevet-Major
Dalzell; and landing at Gravesend in April following,
marched from thence to Canterbury, from whence four
companies were afterwards detached to Dover.

In August the regiment was supplied with new
Percussion Arms. In December it marched to London,
and proceeded from thence by railway to Winchester.

Leaving Winchester in April, 1842, the regiment 1842
proceeded by railway to Gosport, and in August it was
removed to Portsmouth.

On the 22nd of September NEW COLOURS were presented to the regiment, on Southsea Common, by the
Honorable LADY PAKENHAM; the Rev. RICHARD
BINGHAM conducted the ceremony of consecration; and
the regiment was afterwards addressed by Major-
General the Honorable SIR HERCULES R. PAKENHAM,
K.C.B., commanding the South-west District, who
detailed, in a very impressive manner, the ancient
achievements of the corps. A large assemblage of
nobility and gentry were present at the ceremony, and
were afterwards entertained by the officers at a déjeuné
and ball.

The regiment proceeded from Portsmouth to Man- 1843
chester, in May, 1843, and from thence to Ireland in
July. During the remainder of the year it was
stationed at Newbridge and Birr.

From Birr the regiment marched, in February, 1844, 1844
to Naas, and in March removed to Dublin, where it
remained until December, when the regiment proceeded to Cork.

In June, 1845, the SIXTEENTH regiment marched to 1845
Buttevant, and in October to Cork, for the purpose of
proceeding on foreign service.

D

34 THE BEDFORDSHIRE REGIMENT OF FOOT.

1846 The service companies of the regiment, under the command of Lieut.-Colonel Henry McManus, embarked at Cork for Gibraltar, on the 17th and 19th January, 1846, in the freight ships Cressy and Earl Grey, and arrived at Gibraltar on the 11th February. The depôt companies marched from Buttevant to Birr, in April, 1846, and proceeded in November to Fermoy.

1847 On the 9th of March, 1847, the regiment, under the command of Lieut.-Colonel McManus, embarked in Her Majesty's ship Belleisle for Corfu, where it arrived on the 27th March; and on its embarkation for the Ionian Islands, a favourable report was received by the Adjutant-General from the Governor of Gibraltar, General Sir Robert Wilson, who stated, that the corps was " *very efficient and soldier-like,*" and that it was " *distinguished by very commendable conduct throughout its* " *service in the garrison.*"

The depôt companies marched from Fermoy to Youghal in September, 1847.

1848 Lieut.-Colonel McManus retired on half-pay on the 10th March, 1848, and Major Robert Luxmoore was promoted to the rank of Lieut.-Colonel; Captain Charles Grey succeeded to the Majority.

In April, 1848, the depôt companies proceeded to Cork, and embarked for Guernsey on the 4th May, where they are now stationed.

On the 1st June, 1848, the date to which the Record has been continued, the service companies were stationed at Corfu, under the command of Lieut.-Colonel Robert Luxmoore.

1848

SIXTEENTH REGIMENT.
QUEEN'S COLOUR.

REGIMENTAL COLOUR.

FOR CANNON'S MILITARY RECORDS

[35]

SUCCESSION OF COLONELS

OF

THE SIXTEENTH,

OR

THE BEDFORDSHIRE REGIMENT OF FOOT.

ARCHIBALD DOUGLAS,
Appointed 9th October, 1688.

ARCHIBALD DOUGLAS was many years an officer in the First, or the Royal regiment of foot, with which corps he served in France and Germany, when that veteran Scots regiment was in the service of Louis XIV.; but it was withdrawn from the army of the French monarch in 1678, from which period it has been on the British establishment. He was captain of one of the companies of the Royal regiment sent to the relief of Tangier, in Africa, when that fortress was besieged by the Moors in 1680, and he was wounded in the general engagement on the 27th of September, 1680, when the Moorish army was overthrown. He was subsequently promoted to the lieutenant-colonelcy of his regiment; and he commanded the companies of his corps at the battle of Sedgemoor, on the 6th of July, 1685, where he distinguished himself. King James II. placed great confidence in the loyalty of Colonel Douglas, and when His Majesty's power was menaced by the armament under the Prince of Orange, the King nominated this distinguished Scots officer to raise a regiment, now the SIXTEENTH foot, of which he was appointed colonel. At the Revolution in 1688, he withdrew from the service, and was not afterwards employed under the British crown. In consequence of a mark on his countenance, he was sometimes called *Spot*.

SUCCESSION OF COLONELS.

ROBERT HODGES,

Appointed 31*st December*, 1688.

THIS Officer served with the army of Louis XIV. in Germany, as ensign and lieutenant in the Royal regiment of foot, and in 1678, when a grenadier company was added to the regiment, it was placed under his orders, and he was promoted to the rank of captain. The Scots grenadiers under his orders were selected to proceed to the relief of Tangier, and in an account of an action on the 20th of September, 1680, with the Moorish lancers, it is recorded—" The grenadiers, under Captain " Hodges, behaved themselves very bravely." He also distinguished himself in a skirmish on the 22nd of September; and in the general attack on the Moorish lines, on the 27th of that month, he led the assault at the head of his grenadiers, and evinced great gallantry. He was subsequently promoted to the majority of the Royal regiment, and in December, 1688, the Prince of Orange conferred on him the colonelcy of the corps which is now the SIXTEENTH regiment. He served the campaign of 1689, in the Netherlands, under Prince Waldeck, and evinced great courage and ability in command of a detachment of infantry placed in front of the confederate army at Walcourt, when attacked by the French, under Marshal d'Humieres, on the 25th of August. He served the campaigns of 1691 and 1692, under King William III., and was killed by a cannon-ball at the battle of Steenkirk, on the 3rd of August, 1692.

THE HONORABLE JAMES STANLEY,

Appointed 1*st August*, 1692.

THE HONORABLE JAMES STANLEY, third son of Charles eighth Earl of Derby, was an adherent of the principles of the Revolution of 1688, and a member of the Convention of Parliament which conferred the crown on the Prince and Princess of Orange. He procured a commission in the first foot guards, in which corps he obtained the rank of captain and lieut.-colonel; he served several campaigns in Flanders under King William III., and on 1st August, 1692, His Majesty, in his camp at Lambeque, promoted him, from lieutenant-colonel of the foot guards, to the command of the SIXTEENTH regiment of foot, in succession to Colonel Hodges, who was killed at the battle of Steenkirk. He was also one of the grooms of the bed-chamber to King William III. On the decease of his brother, in 1702, he succeeded to the dignity of Earl of Derby. On the 10th June, 1702, he was constituted Lord-Lieutenant of North Wales and of the County of Lancaster; and in the following year he had a patent to be Vice-Admiral of the said County during Queen Anne's reign. The Earl of Derby resigned his military appointments in 1705, and on 10th June, 1706, was sworn at Windsor, by her Majesty's command, one of the Privy Council, and at the same time Chancellor of the Duchy of Lancaster. At her Majesty's coronation, on 23rd April, 1702, he carried one of the Three Swords of State, as he did also at the coronation of King George I., on the 20th October, 1714. At the change of the administration in 1710, he was removed from his posts, and from that of Lord-Lieutenant of the County of Lancaster, but was again constituted Lord-Lieutenant of that County on the 5th August, 1714. On 23rd September, 1715, he was appointed Captain of the Yeomen of the Guard. He died at Knowsley, on Sunday, 1st February, 1736.

FRANCIS GODFREY,

Appointed 25th May, 1705.

THIS officer was nephew to the great Duke of Marlborough;* he held a commission in the foot guards, in the time of King William III., and was promoted to captain and lieut.-colonel, and he served several campaigns in the Netherlands under his uncle. In 1705 he was promoted to the colonelcy of the SIXTEENTH regiment, and in 1710 he was advanced to the rank of brigadier-general; in 1711 he disposed of the colonelcy of the regiment. He died on the 6th of October, 1712.

---

* Francis Godfrey was the son of Charles Godfrey, Esq., who married Miss Arabella Churchill, mistress of King James II., and mother of James Duke of Berwick. Miss Arabella Churchill was the sister of John Lord Churchill, afterwards Duke of Marlborough.

HENRY DURELL,

Appointed 17th February, 1711.

THIS officer held a commission in the foot guards, in which corps he rose to the rank of captain and lieut.-colonel. He served at several battles and sieges in the Netherlands and in Germany, under the great Duke of Marlborough, and was promoted to the rank of brigadier-general in 1710: in 1711 he obtained the colonelcy of the SIXTEENTH regiment. He commanded a brigade in Flanders, in 1712, and was appointed Deputy Governor of Dunkirk, when that fortress was delivered up to the British troops. He died on the 1st of December, 1712.

HANS HAMILTON,

Appointed 23rd June, 1713.

HANS HAMILTON was many years an officer of the SIXTEENTH regiment, of which corps he was appointed lieut.-colonel, and he served three campaigns under the great Duke of Marlborough. His meritorious conduct on all occasions was rewarded, in 1705, with the colonelcy of the Thirty-fourth regiment, which corps he accompanied to Spain, and served as quartermaster-general under the Earl of Peterborough at the capture of Barcelona, &c. He was promoted to the rank of brigadier-general in 1710, and commanded a brigade in Flanders at the forcing of the French lines at Arleux, and at the siege of Bouchain in 1711. In 1713 he was removed to the SIXTEENTH regiment, but he withdrew from the service in 1715, selling his commission. He died in 1721.

RICHARD VISCOUNT IRWIN,

Appointed 11th July, 1715.

RICHARD INGRAM, Baron Ingram, and VISCOUNT IRWIN, commenced his military service in the life guards, in which corps he rose to the rank of lieutenant and lieut.-colonel, and was afterwards lieut.-colonel of the SIXTEENTH regiment, of which corps he was appointed colonel in 1715; at the same time he was nominated Governor of Hull. In 1717 he was removed to the second horse, now first dragoon guards, and three years afterwards he was nominated Governor of Barbadoes; but previous to his embarkation he was taken ill of the small-pox, of which he died on the 10th of April, 1721.

JAMES CHOLMELEY,

Appointed 13th December, 1717.

JAMES CHOLMELEY was many years an officer of reputation in the SIXTEENTH regiment, to the lieut.-colonelcy of which corps he was promoted by King George I., in consideration of his service in Flanders under the Duke of Marlborough, and his excellent conduct on all occasions. In 1717 he was promoted to the colonelcy of the regiment. He died in 1724.

HENRY, EARL OF DELORAINE, K.B.,

Appointed 7th April, 1724.

LORD HENRY SCOTT, third son of James Duke of Monmouth and Anne Duchess of Buccleuch, obtained a commission in the army in the reign of William III.; he served with reputation in the reign of Queen Anne, obtained the command of one of the newly-raised regiments of foot in 1704; and on the 29th of March, 1706, he was created Baron Scott of Goldielands, Viscount Hermitage, and EARL OF DELORAINE. He supported the treaty of union between England and Scotland and other measures of the court; in 1715 he was chosen one of the sixteen representatives of the Scottish peerage; and was re-chosen in 1722, and again in 1727. His regiment having been disbanded at the peace of Utrecht, he was appointed, on the 1st of June, 1715, colonel of the second, or Scots troop of horse grenadier guards, which he held two years. In 1724 he obtained the colonelcy of the SIXTEENTH foot; he was invested with the order of the Bath on its revival in 1725; and promoted to the rank of major-general in 1726. He was removed to the seventh horse, now sixth dragoon guards, or carabineers, in July, 1730. He died on the 25th of December following.

ROGER HANDASYD,

Appointed 9th July, 1730.

THIS Officer obtained a commission in a regiment of foot in 1694, and served two campaigns under King William III. He also served with reputation in the wars of Queen Anne, and succeeded his father in the colonelcy of the Twenty-second regiment in 1712; in 1730 he was removed to the SIXTEENTH regiment. He was promoted to the rank of major-general in 1739, and to that of lieut.-general in 1743. He died in 1763.

THE HONORABLE ROBERT BRUDENELL.

Appointed 14th June, 1763.

THE HONORABLE ROBERT BRUDENELL, third son of George Earl of Cardigan, was many years a member of Parliament for Marlborough, also groom of the bed-chamber to His Royal Highness the Duke of York, whose train he bore at the coronation of King George III. He was appointed captain and lieut.-colonel in the third foot guards, in 1758; promoted to the colonelcy of the SIXTEENTH in 1763, and removed to the fourth, or King's Own regiment, in 1765. He died at Windsor, in October, 1768.

SIR WILLIAM DRAPER, K.B.

Appointed 25th June, 1765.

WILLIAM DRAPER was educated at Eton, and at King's College, Cambridge, for the Church: but preferring the profession of arms, he went to the East Indies, and was employed in the service of the Honorable the East India Company. He subsequently obtained a commission from the King, and on the 2nd of November, 1757, he was promoted to lieut.-colonel commandant of the seventy-ninth regiment, then raised, with which corps he served in India, and acquired the reputation of a brave and meritorious officer. He returned to England in 1760, and in 1761 he commanded a brigade at the capture of Belleisle. He again proceeded to India, and commanded the land forces of the expedition which captured Manilla in 1763. His regiment was disbanded soon afterwards; and in 1765 King George III. conferred upon him the colonelcy of the SIXTEENTH regiment, from which he exchanged, in 1766, to the late 121st regiment. In 1769 he appeared in a literary character, and answered some of Junius's letters; and in the autumn of the same year he proceeded to South Carolina. He was promoted to the rank of major-general in 1772; to that of lieut.-general in 1777; he was honoured with the dignity of a Knight of the Bath, and nominated Governor of Yarmouth. He died in 1787.

JAMES GISBORNE,

Appointed 4th March, 1766.

AFTER a progressive service in the subordinate commissions, this officer was appointed lieut.-colonel of the tenth regiment in 1755, and he was afterwards employed many years on the staff of Ireland, as quartermaster-general in that country. In 1762 he was promoted to the colonelcy of the 121st regiment; and in 1766 he was removed to the SIXTEENTH regiment. He was promoted to the rank of major-general in 1770, and to that of lieut.-general in 1777. He died in 1778.

JAMES ROBERTSON,

Appointed 14th May, 1778.

THIS Officer entered the army in the reign of King George II.; he served in America during the seven years' war, and held the appointment of deputy-Quartermaster-general, with the rank of lieut.-colonel, under Lieut.-General Sir Jeffrey (afterwards Lord) Amherst, who completed the conquest of Canada in 1760. In the same year Lieut.-Colonel Robertson was appointed to the fifteenth regiment, and in 1768 he was removed to the SIXTEENTH, which corps he commanded in Florida several years. On the breaking out of the American war, he was again called into active service in that country, and in January, 1776, he was appointed colonel commandant of the second battalion of the sixtieth regiment, and promoted to the local rank of major-general in America: in 1777 he obtained the rank of major-general, and in 1778 the colonelcy of the SIXTEENTH regiment. His services in the

American war were rewarded with the appointment of Governor of New York ; and in 1782 he was promoted to the rank of Lieut.-General. He died on the 4th of March, 1788.

THE HONORABLE THOMAS BRUCE,

Appointed 6th March, 1788.

THE HONORABLE THOMAS BRUCE, son of William Earl of Kincardine, choosing the profession of arms, rose to the commission of major in the sixtieth regiment in 1768, and in 1770 he was promoted to the lieut.-colonelcy of the sixty-fifth regiment, which corps he commanded in North America during the early part of the American war. In 1781 he was appointed lieut.-colonel commandant of the 100th regiment, with which corps he served in the East Indies, and obtained the local rank of major-general in that country in March, 1782: in November following he was promoted to the rank of major-general. After the termination of the war with Tippoo Saib, the ruler of the Mysore, the 100th regiment was disbanded, and in 1788 Major-General the Honorable Thomas Bruce was appointed colonel of the SIXTEENTH regiment: in 1796 he was promoted to the rank of lieut.-general. He died in 1797.

HENRY BOWYER,

Appointed 15th December, 1797.

THIS officer entered the army in 1771, and after serving five years in the sixty-eighth regiment, he was promoted captain in the nineteenth, and in 1778 he was removed to the sixty-sixth : his distinguished services during the American war were rewarded with the rank of lieut.-colonel in November 1782. In 1787 he was appointed major, and in 1787 lieut.-colonel of the sixty-sixth regiment. He served in the West Indies, was promoted to the rank of major-general in 1795, and to that of lieut.-general, 1802. In March, 1797, he was appointed colonel of the eighty-ninth regiment, and was removed, in December following, to the SIXTEENTH. He held the appointment of commander of the forces in the Windward and Leeward Islands. His decease occurred in 1808.

Sir Charles Green, Bart.,

Appointed 29th August, 1808.

Charles Green entered the army as gentleman cadet in the Royal Artillery in 1760; in 1765 he was appointed ensign in the thirty-first regiment, which corps he joined at Pensacola in 1766. In 1768 he was employed on a particular service at New Orleans and on the Mississippi river; and in 1771 he served as engineer at the Bahama Islands. He joined his regiment at St. Vincent in 1772, and served against the Caribs; but returned to England in 1773, and was promoted to a lieutenancy; and in 1774 to captain in the thirty-first regiment. Proceeding to America in 1776, he was nominated aide-de-camp to Major-General Phillips, and served the campaign of 1777 in that capacity. He was wounded at Freeman's Farm in September of that year, and returning to England in 1778, he was appointed aide-de-camp to Lieut.-General Sir Adolphus Oughton, commander-in-chief in North Britain. Having joined the thirty-first in Canada, in May, 1780, he was soon afterwards nominated major of brigade to the Montreal district. In 1783 he obtained the rank of major in the army, and the majority of his regiment in 1788. On the breaking out of the war in 1793, he was promoted to the lieut.-colonelcy of a battalion formed of independent companies, and in 1794 he exchanged to the thirtieth regiment. After serving two years at Corsica, he was nominated civil governor of Grenada, and was promoted to the rank of colonel in 1797. His eye-sight having been injured by the climate of Grenada, he returned to England in 1801 : in 1803 he was appointed brigadier-general on the Staff of Ireland, and was afterwards removed to England; he was knighted in May of this year, and promoted to the rank of major-general in September. In 1804 he was nominated colonel of the York Light Infantry Volunteers; and afterwards proceeding to the West Indies, he assembled an armament and captured the Dutch Settlements of Surinam in South America. He remained at Surinam a year, and returned to England in 1805 : in 1807 he was advanced to the dignity of a baronet, and in 1808 appointed colonel of the sixteenth regiment. He commanded the garrison of Malta some time; was promoted to the rank of lieut.-general in 1809 ; removed to the thirty-seventh regiment in 1814; and advanced to the rank of general in 1819. He died in 1831.

Sir George Prevost, Bart.,

Appointed 17th February, 1814.

George Prevost was appointed ensign in the sixtieth regiment in 1779, lieutenant in the forty-seventh in 1782, and captain in the sixtieth in 1783; in 1784 he was removed to the twenty-fifth regiment, with which corps he served at Gibraltar, and in 1790 he was promoted to a majority in the sixtieth. Early in 1794 he took command of the third battalion of the sixtieth at Antigua; he was promoted to a lieut.-colonelcy in his regiment in March, and in 1795 he was employed at St. Vincent's in suppressing the insurrection of the Caribs, and in resisting the French invasion: he commanded a column at the reduction of La Vigie. In October he was directed to assume the command of the troops at Dominica; but he returned to the third battalion of the sixtieth at St. Vincent's, in January, 1796, and was twice severely wounded in opposing the progress of the enemy towards the capital. Returning to England in consequence of his wounds, he was employed a short time as an inspecting field-officer; having been promoted to the rank of colonel on the 1st of January, 1796. He was subsequently nominated brigadier-general in the West Indies; he commanded the troops at Barbadoes, afterwards at St. Lucia, where he was appointed lieut.-governor; but returned to England after the peace of Amiens in 1802. Four months afterwards he was nominated Governor of Dominica; and in 1803 he served as second in command at the reduction of St. Lucia and Tobago: for a short time he commanded the troops in the Windward and Leeward Islands. In 1804 he successfully defended Dominica against a French armament; and was promoted to the rank of major-general in 1805, when he returned to England and was appointed lieut.-governor of Portsmouth. He proceeded to Nova Scotia in 1808, with the local rank of lieut.-general; and in 1809 he distinguished himself as second in command at the reduction of Martinique. Returning afterwards to Nova Scotia, he obtained the appointment of com-

SUCCESSION OF COLONELS. 45

mander in-chief in Canada. He was advanced to the dignity of a BARONET for his distinguished services in the West Indies. In 1811 he was promoted to the rank of lieut.-general; and he was nominated captain-general and governor-in-chief in North America. War having commenced with the United States, he defended the Canadas successfully nearly three years, under circumstances of peculiar difficulty. In February, 1814, he was appointed colonel of the SIXTEENTH regiment. After an unsuccessful attack on the American post at Plattsburg, he was recalled to England; where he died in January, 1816.

HUGH MACKAY GORDON,

Appointed 8th January, 1816.

HUGH MACKAY GORDON entered the army during the American war, and was many years an officer of the SIXTEENTH regiment, with which corps he served in Florida, South Carolina, and Georgia, also in Nova Scotia and the West Indies. He was promoted captain in the SIXTEENTH in 1788, major in the army in 1796; lieut.-colonel in the army in 1798; and obtained a majority in his regiment in 1799; at the peace of Amiens he was placed on half-pay. He was promoted to the rank of major-general in 1811, and was nominated colonel of the York Chasseurs in 1814; in 1816 he was removed to the SIXTEENTH, with which regiment he had previously performed much service. In 1821 he was promoted to the rank of lieut.-general. He died in 1823.

WILLIAM CARR, VISCOUNT BERESFORD, G.C.B., G.C.H.,

Appointed 15th March, 1823.

www.ingramcontent.com/pod-product-compliance
Lightning Source LLC
Chambersburg PA
CBHW020019050426
42450CB00005B/555